Saving the Oceans

Written by Kerrie Shanahan

Series Consultant: Linda Hoyt

WorldWise™
Content-based Learning

Contents

Introduction

Oceans are important. Many animals live in oceans, and on the land near oceans. Many people need fish and other sea animals for food.

But the oceans of the world are at risk.

Our amazing oceans are at risk because of things people are doing. We are polluting the oceans. We are taking too many fish from the oceans. And we are damaging ocean habitats.

We know why our oceans are at risk. But what can we do to save them?

Chapter 1

Why are the oceans polluted?

People are polluting the oceans with rubbish, **waste** and chemicals such as oil.

People drop rubbish

If people drop rubbish on the beach or from boats, they pollute the oceans. If rubbish is dropped in city streets, it can be washed down drains and end up in the oceans.

Rubbish can kill sea animals if they mistake it for food and eat it, or if they become **tangled** in it.

Lots of plastic ends up in the oceans. Plastic stays in the occans for a long time because it takes thousands of years to break down.

Did you know?

Scientists predict that by the year 2050, there will be more pieces of plastic in the oceans than fish!

What can people do?

- Always put rubbish in bins.
- Buy things that have less plastic packaging.
- Stop using plastic shopping bags.
- Stop using plastic drink bottles, straws and utensils.
- Recycle as much plastic and other waste as possible.

People put waste in the oceans

Waste, such as oil used at home, can be washed into drains
and carried into rivers.

Chemical waste from factories is sometimes put into rivers.
Chemicals used on farms can be washed into rivers, and
the rivers carry the waste and chemicals into the oceans.

Oil spills into the oceans

Oil can be spilled from ships if oil tankers crash onto a reef or into another ship.

If cars drip oil onto roads, the oil gets washed down drains and can end up in the oceans.

When oil gets into the oceans, it can kill sea animals and destroy their homes.

Cleaning a bird covered in oil.

Find out more

One of the largest oil spills happened in 2010 in the Gulf of Mexico. Find out more about this terrible accident.

What can people do?
- Don't let household waste get into rivers.
- Separate chemicals, oils and paints from other household rubbish collections.

Chapter 2

What is happening to sea animals?

Millions of fish and sea animals are taken from the ocean to feed people all around the world. Now some fish and sea animals are in danger of becoming extinct.

People catch too many fish

We don't eat all the fish that we catch, so some fish are wasted. They are tossed back into the ocean, where they often die after being **injured** in the catch.

Some fish grow very slowly. They take many years to start breeding. If too many fish are taken from the ocean, there may not be enough fish left to **breed**.

What can people do?

- Protect areas from fishing where fish are in danger of extinction.
- Set up fish farms that breed fish for people to eat.
- Set aside places in the ocean where fish can breed.

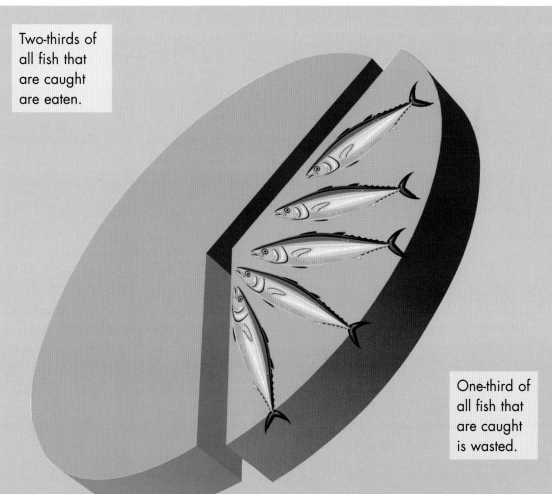

Two-thirds of all fish that are caught are eaten.

One-third of all fish that are caught is wasted.

11

People catch animals they don't want

Some people use large nets to catch fish. These large fishing nets also trap other fish and sea animals that people don't want to eat.

Turtles, seals, dolphins and birds are sometimes caught in these nets. Many of these animals are thrown back into the ocean, but they often die because they have already been injured.

People kill whales

Long ago, thousands of whales were hunted and killed. Today, some types of whales are endangered. Whaling is now banned almost everywhere in the world, but some people still hunt and kill whales to sell their meat.

What can people do?

- Buy seafood that is caught in a way that protects the oceans.
- Stop using large nets that catch sea animals such as turtles and dolphins.

Find out more

Whales were once widely hunted. Find out how people used certain parts of the whale.

Chapter 3

What is happening to ocean habitats?

People are damaging ocean habitats where many sea animals live.

People damage the ocean floor

The **ocean floor** is a place where many sea animals and plants make their home. The ocean floor helps keep the ocean healthy.

Some fishing boats use dragnets to catch fish. Dragnets are nets that are dragged behind a boat. When they are used on the bottom of the ocean, they disturb the places where many sea animals and plants live.

The ocean floor can take a long time to recover after it has been damaged.

What can people do?

- Don't disturb the ocean floor.
- Stop fishing with dragnets on the ocean floor.
- Protect certain places from fishing.

People damage reefs and rock pools

Many sea animals live around **reefs** and in **rock pools**. When people walk on reefs and in rock pools, they can damage **marine habitats**. If people take things from rock pools or reefs, that can also damage the ocean.

If rubbish is left on a beach, it can wash into rock pools, or the tide can carry it out to reefs. Rubbish in rock pools or on reefs pollutes the water, and this dirty water can make the animals that live in those habitats sick.

If reefs and rock pools are damaged, it can take many years for them to recover.

Find out more

Ocean temperatures are rising. Find out how this affects the animals that live on reefs and in rock pools.

What can people do?

- Don't take sea creatures home.
- Look at animals in rock pools but don't touch them.
- Be careful where you walk when visiting rock pools.

Conclusion

Our oceans are at risk. But there are many things we can do to help save them.

We can stop putting waste and rubbish in the oceans, we can take fewer fish from the oceans and we can protect ocean habitats.

If we all work together, we will save our oceans.

Glossary

breed   to have offspring

injured   hurt or broken

marine habitats   places where groups of sea animals or plants usually live

ocean floor   the land at the bottom of the sea

reefs   long chains of coral that are just under the surface of the seawater

rock pools   pools of seawater found on the rocky shore of a beach after the tide has gone out

tangled   twisted together in a way that is difficult to undo

waste   rubbish such as plastic, metal, oil, chemicals and sewage

Index